H.B. Morse

~

Customs Commissioner

and

Historian of China

H.B. MORSE

~

Customs Commissioner
and
Historian of China

John King Fairbank
Martha Henderson Coolidge
Richard J. Smith

THE UNIVERSITY PRESS OF KENTUCKY

of the household might then be sold. Boys could be taken in and adopted by families that needed sons, while wives and daughters had some value as slaves or prostitutes. And when famine had finally destroyed the things most dear to every householder and parent, the last recourse was cannibalism. As people fell dead by the roadside, their flesh had to be quickly carved off and carried away, before wild dogs or birds of prey could get at the bodies. The Roman Catholic bishop of Shansi, Monsignor Louis Monagatta, reported in March 1877: "Now they kill the living to have them for food. Husbands eat their wives. Parents eat their sons and daughters, and children eat their parents." Gruesome stories began to circulate freely—of a grandson who chopped his grandmother to pieces, of a niece who boiled and ate her aunt.[15]

Under these nightmarish circumstances, the foreign communities at Chefoo, Tientsin, Shanghai, and other ports began to collect relief funds for forwarding to missionaries. Some 36,000 taels thus reached Chefoo to help counter the famine in Shantung. In June 1877 Governor-general Li Hung-chang reported to Peking a collection of 214,000 taels from officials and gentry in that province. In October 1877 the Chinese secretary at the British Legation, William F. Mayers, put the total recorded relief funds in both money and goods at 2,623,000 taels, including the foreigners' 36,000 taels.[16] By this time, however, the dead already totaled several million persons. Appropriation of government funds was at best a gesture of sincerity, to show the emperor cared.[17] The foreign contributions, though of great symbolic value, were practically inconsequential.

Moreover, collecting money from foreigners was the easy part of famine relief. Getting funds securely delivered to the heads of destitute families required penetration of the countryside to the household level, bypassing layers of yamen underlings, village headmen, and the leaders of the local mutual security system known as *pao-chia,* through whom top-level decisions were usually conveyed. This in turn required hard travel by sampan, cart, chair, or mule or on foot such as only missionaries, bandits, or soldiers ever attempted. The Reverend John L. Nevius provides us with an inspirational example. In the period from March 10 to June 4, 1877, he disbursed a total of 7,600 silver taels in relief funds. Having enrolled the names of the destitute in various villages, he sent to each enrollee fifty copper cash (one-sixtieth of a tael under the circumstances; normally one-twentieth of a tael) every five days and so aided 32,500 persons in 383 villages within a ten- to fifteen-mile radius. The coppers enabled them to buy grain to mix with the leaves, roots, and chaff or even slate-stone that they were eating. Nevius's greatest problem was sending the silver he had received to market towns twenty-five to forty miles away to purchase cash and wheel it back in barrows.[18]

Relief work was not only difficult; it was also dangerous. The greatest threat, aside from banditry, came from the mob-sized numbers of the destitute. Hordes of homeless, starving people congregated on the main routes of travel. As Commissioner Detring at Tientsin explained to the Shanghai Relief Committee, the Chinese authorities had to stop giving relief near Tientsin because "the masses of relief seekers swamped on more than one occasion the distribution office and compelled the relief agents to save themselves over the wall or through a back gate."[19] We may compare the incident in Theodore H. White's *Mountain Road,* where a well-meaning dispenser of food is killed in the melée his food arouses.[20]

Morse's Role in Famine Relief

Morse's introduction to the suffering caused by famine must have been the influx of desperate refugees who flocked into Tientsin during his first year there. In the winter of 1877 the *North China Herald* reported ninety thousand refugees. There were thirty deaths after dark every day, seventy to eighty when it was cold. One harsh January night, a terrible fire in a dangerously located soup kitchen killed about three thousand people.[21]

In the summer of 1878, after many months of exhausting effort, the Tientsin Relief Committee decided to send five thousand taels to be distributed in Hsien-hsien, an area known to foreigners as an established center of Catholic mission work.[22] It was located in Ho-chien prefecture of Chihli province, about seventy-five miles from Tientsin. Morse tells us that "someone was wanted to take relief into Hokien-fu who should be acceptable to both Reverend Muirhead, the Secretary of the Shanghai Relief Committee and Viceroy Li Hung-chang, and Detring proposed [Edmond] Farago and me. Farago soon withdrew and I was left alone."[23] It says a great deal for Morse's character and personality that he was one of two Customs assistants who were deputed to help distribute famine relief funds, particularly since the relief effort had recently been stigmatized by charges of corruption.

When Morse went on his mission into southeastern Chihli province, he traveled through the North China plain on its eastern side. The plain has a diameter of some five hundred miles, from the sea south of Tientsin to the mountain ranges of Shansi province and from the Great Wall southward to the Huai River basin. While these boundaries are indistinct, a characteristic of the whole region is that it is a drainage area in which water from the mountainous west makes its way toward the coast. The region has a number of watercourses, both rivers and canals, and along the route where Morse made his trip there was still no lack of water for daily necessities or even for transport on canals. The problem was inadequate rainfall for crops. Using muscle power on treadle pumps to lift irrigation water onto fields could not make up for the lack of rain. The fields were dry, parched, and unproductive.

Morse and Farago set out on June 27, 1878, but met continual delays. First, the carts promised by an official arrived only at 8:00 P.M.—too late to go on. Second, once started, it took three hours to cover eighteen *li* (about six miles) to a certain dam where boats had been requisitioned by the soldiers who accompanied the party. A victim of typhus was claimed to be aboard one boat, but the malady proved to be only indigestion; a second boat had only a fourteen-year-old boy left on board, though Morse noted that he "turned out to be the best boatman of the lot"; and the third boat "had accidentally lost nearly all her flooring planks." They added a fourth boat (a *ts'ao-tzu* or "double-ender") and found volunteers to fill out the crews, each presumably three persons. We may assume the party included one or two minor officials, soldiers, a cook, and personal servants, as well as luggage. Morse and Farago's boat was under the direction of two men and an old woman.[24]

The next twenty-eight hours took them through an "inland sea," one of the lakes below Tientsin on the swampy east coast of Chihli. Banks appeared—about two miles distant on either side—and in one area they followed a channel five to ten feet wide through rushes. Eventually they began to ascend a fast-flowing river and passed under a dozen low bridges, at each of which the mat housing on the boats had to be carefully taken down. On the fifth day they arrived within a mile of Ho-chien fu and "went in a drenching rain" to call on the prefect. "He received us well and promised to send carts to convey us to Hsien-hsien." This cart trip took about eight hours.[25]

Morse and Farago were under orders to find the provincial relief commissioner, Sheng Hsüan-huai, a key member of Li Hung-chang's team of young administrators already active in a variety of modernization projects.[26] At the age of thirty-four, Sheng held the rank of a taotai waiting-to-be-appointed (*hou-pu tao*). Sheng was a rising star in Li's industrial empire, as we shall see. On July 4 he came north forty-five miles from Ching-chou to Hsien-hsien to discuss with Morse and Farago "the advisability of distributing cash instead of silver." The five thousand taels' worth of silver

Club still supplied Western-style theater, and adventuresome foreigners always had opportunities to explore the Chinese city and its environs. In early 1887 Nan Morse herself organized an "expedition" with Mrs. Drew and others to visit the Lung-hua Pagoda. We can be certain, however, that she and her friends did not mingle with the locals or stay very long.[3] As always, Chinese life and culture remained a separate world.

Morse's first assignment at Shanghai was to establish new Customs bonding procedures. He had begun to work on the "bonded godown question" while still in the service of the CMSN Company but "had to drop it" in the midst of his battle with Sheng Hsüan-huai and Shen Neng-hu.[4] According to Western practice, goods imported in bond could be held in storage before being released upon payment of duty; or, if going further, they could be shipped out again without any duty payment. This was a privilege already enjoyed in most of the rest of the world and long sought by Western merchants in the Chinese treaty ports. But in China, bonding had never worked out.

Part of the difficulty lay in the complex structure of taxes and duties. Import duty and transit passes were paid to Customs. After expenses had been subtracted, funds were forwarded to the central government in Peking. Likin, however, was a provincial tax that was collected at stations on trade routes and designated for local officials. Naturally, these officials did not want to see likin payments circumvented by having goods travel under Customs transit passes. The Chinese Customs superintendents, for their part, had vested interests in maintaining their job of receiving the duties paid by foreign merchants to the Customs bank at each port. They wanted assurances that goods once imported would sooner or later be liable for regular duties.[5] Hart's establishment of a bonding system in 1887 consequently required diplomatic as well as procedural skills. It fell to Morse to work out arrangements that would, among other things, meet the concerns of the Chinese superintendents of customs.

Morse had made a special study of British and Western European bonding while in the London office and had carried on his research in New York while on leave during the winter of 1882–83. With that training and his China Merchants' Company experience, he was in a good position to understand the problems involved in bonding in China. Hart had visited Shanghai as early as 1882 to canvass the possibilities, and in October 1887 he promoted Morse (whose Customs rank was then second assistant A) to be deputy commissioner for bonding in the Shanghai office. According to the I.G., "[Morse's] acquaintance with the China Merchants Company's wharves, godowns, vessels and business point to him specially as the fittest person for this post."[6]

Morse was to report for duty before mid-November. With his "energy and intelligence" (as Hart put it), he would arrange for bonding procedures to commence on January 1, 1888. The new Bonding Desk in the expansive Shanghai Customshouse would, in turn, maintain contact with "various other desks—Import, Export, Duty Memo, Clearance, etc." It would also deal with "the opium work." Hart indicated that Morse should have an assistant at the Bonding Desk so as to "be free to visit opium hulks, opium godowns and bonded warehouses whenever necessary."[7]

The British and Chinese governments had agreed to the Additional Article on Opium on July 18, 1885. It was "additional" to the Chefoo Convention of 1876, the third Anglo-Chinese treaty settlement (after 1842–43 and 1858–60) that completed the main structure of imperialist privilege in China. Now in 1885, a capstone had been put on the impairment of Chinese sovereignty. Under this Additional Article, imported foreign opium was to be stored in bonded warehouses or receiving hulks under Customs control at the port of entry. It could be released only after payment of thirty taels per chest as Customs tariff duty and not over eighty taels as likin, paid to Chinese provincial officials. Only then could it pass through the interior under a Customs transit certificate free of further taxation. In the short term this was a gain for China's central government (via the Customs), which thus replaced, at least with respect to opium, the inland likin fees that had formerly been under dispute with local authorities.[8]

All this was easily said, but Morse had to devise complex procedures to take account of multiple alternatives. General cargo goods released from bond were subject to duty if they were for sale at Shanghai or the Yangtze ports, but no duty was paid if they were exported to other ports under exemption or drawback certificates issued to foreign vessels permitted to carry both foreign and Chinese goods. Morse devised twelve different forms (to be printed in red for identification), and applicants took the steps appropriate to their needs by going from one desk to another within the customshouse. This system exemplified the division of customs procedure among different component desks, where each customer could pursue his own mixture for his own requirements.[9]

If properly carried out, the procedures would have been foolproof, but of course Shanghai was still Shanghai. Contrary to the Customs Service's intention and desire, bonding at once became monopolized at the China Merchants' Company's warehouses. In the absence of competition to keep charges low, the company then raised its prices. As a result of the increased cost and the complexity of the bonding procedure, it was little used by merchants. Thus, during an initial six-month trial period, only 30 of 416 vessels entitled to bond their cargoes took advantage of the privilege; and of the 300,000 packages discharged by these 30 vessels, only about 3 percent were bonded. So matters stood for the next ten years. Out of some eight hundred categories of import goods, only about forty-five appeared in the quarterly and yearly bonding tables published by the Customs Service. Bonding was supposed to preclude payment of duty for goods in storage or in transit, but since low import duties prevailed and goods passed quickly from consignee to dealer, there was little incentive for merchants to take the time and effort that bonding required.[10]

In short, under Chinese conditions, bonding as a general practice failed.[11] On the other hand, bonding for opium imports under the Additional Article proceeded smoothly, the parties involved, like Jardine, being on the whole respectable and responsible. After a maximum import in 1879, however, foreign opium began to give ground to China's domestic production. The figures are striking. In 1888 Indian and Persian opium imported into China totaled 82,612 piculs (one picul equals about 133 pounds); by 1897 the total was less than 50,000 piculs. Although foreign importers blamed the decline on the high likin tax allowed by the Additional Article, the fundamental cause was clearly the increased production and growing popularity of cheaper native opium.[12]

After discharging his responsibilities as deputy commissioner for bonding, Morse entered another realm of administrative complexity when he became assistant statistical secretary at Shanghai in 1888. This rapidly growing branch of the Customs Service, where Morse would eventually end his career as the head of operations, combined the functions of an archive, a research institute, a government printing office, and a publishing house.[13] Although we do not know precisely what Morse did during his several months as assistant statistical secretary, a preliminary look at the functions of his department may suggest the broad range of his administrative concerns.

The Statistical Department's flow of publications, organized into seven main categories, including six series, was formidable in size and diversity. The first series was called Statistical, and consisted of *Returns of Trade* or *Trade Reports* issued daily, quarterly, annually, and decennially. In the end there were five issues of *Decennial Reports* (for the years 1882–91, 1892–1901, 1902–11, 1912–21, and 1922–31). These symposia summa-

the treaty port of entry to China or of exit into the interior, such levies went entirely to the central government.[36]

The division of tax receipts between the provincial and central authorities paralleled the question of conveyance. As we have seen, ships in international trade were expected to enter only at treaty ports and therefore to be entirely under the jurisdiction of the Maritime Customs. They were not supposed to ship any cargo at other ports, and if they did, they were severely penalized. On the other hand, the Chinese native shipping or junk trade was expected to handle Chinese goods almost entirely, and if these vessels were carrying foreign goods, the products would go under a transit pass. Since junks frequently used non–treaty ports, they often smuggled goods that should have been conveyed under transit passes. There was no inward likin at ports, only somewhat outside them.

The use of steam launches in the shipping world of China required new policies. At Tamsui, for instance, Morse decided that foreign produce reexported in launches would be subject to transit dues and not likin; for Chinese produce, the reverse would be true. Native goods coming into port in launches destined for Chinese ports would pay likin only, while native produce destined for foreign ports would pay transit dues once it had been transferred to foreign ownership. Most inland transit was covered by likin, since goods of Taiwanese origin were generally Chinese-owned until they reached a treaty port. Regarding the choice between likin and transit dues on produce carried by launch to non–treaty ports in Formosa, Morse proposed to the governor that he should collect a single half entry or exit duty and distribute it under "transit dues and likin headings." Fortunately, the governor agreed.[37]

Sometimes likin charges were higher than transit dues, sometimes the reverse. This circumstance provided a temptation to shift between the two for best advantage. The way to do so would be to change the ownership of goods, since tax classification depended on ownership. In order to prevent this from happening, Morse tried to put foreigners and Chinese on the same footing. He did this in the case of tea by substituting for the likin tax "simultaneous collection of full and half duty on all tea shipped." In other words, at all points of entry he mandated the full payment of export duty plus a half-duty payment as a transit duty—the appropriate amount allocated to likin. Morse based his plan on a "full and half duty" scheme proposed by Hart several years earlier but never implemented.[38]

The problem with this idea was that ordinary tea likin yielded to the governor of Taiwan about $350,000 worth of revenue a year, while the half-duty likin would amount to only about $260,000. The governor obviously did not want to absorb this kind of loss. As time passed, Morse came up with additional sources of revenue to make his plan more palatable. But when the scheme began to include non–treaty ports, the governor balked. On the one hand, he worried that he could not "trust the Chinese alone at the sub-ports." On the other, he thought that having foreigners manage duty collection at these places "would make the plan too expensive."[39]

Such problems in the hybrid world of "foreign" and "native" trade were compounded by the peculiar nature of the daily contact between Maritime Customs officials and Chinese functionaries within the local yamen. Morse's relations with the customs superintendent, though steadily maintained, remained largely perfunctory. The man at Tamsui turned out to be a relative of the governor who occupied a sinecure. He had no connection with the likin tax and merely maintained the Chinese Customs Bank into which revenue from Customs duties was paid, to be accounted for by the Customs and ultimately sent to Peking. Morse wrote that the man did practically nothing and was lethargic at what he did.[40] If his account is accurate, we can easily see why the well-intentioned and energetic acting commissioner occasionally became frustrated.

The Discomforts of Home

Morse took responsibility not only for the work of his local staff but also for their general welfare. In all, there were eight foreign members in addition to himself and Nan, and fifty or sixty Chinese. Conditions were less than satisfactory. In the first place, Tamsui's weather left much to be desired. According to one contemporary observer, it was "not healthy even for Chinese, far less for Europeans."[41] Summers were hot and humid; winters tended to be "wet and wind without, damp and mould within."[42] *The Treaty Ports of China and Japan* (1867) indicates that during the rainy season, from late November to early May, "[t]he dampness of the air makes it unpleasantly cold, though the thermometer shows a high figure as compared with the same latitude on the China coast."[43] Periodic typhoons only added to the misery.

To avoid the dampness, some of the Customs housing had already been put on raised piles. This now had to be done for the rest of the quarters. The new harbormaster began to supervise the carpenters' work on the housing. Roofs also needed repair. Furthermore, it seemed essential to put out of action the adjacent rice fields that provided so much dampness to the

Albert David Morse,
Hosea's father, 1880s.
Courtesy of Jean Osborne.

Mercy Dexter Park Morse,
Hosea's mother, 1880s.
Courtesy of Jean Osborne.

of small training schools to produce talent capable of leading in China's military, industrial, agricultural, and intellectual modernization. Fourteen years younger than Li Hung-chang, he was like Li in his utter loyalty and sycophancy toward the Empress Dowager.

The radical reformers of 1898, whose followers inherited the reform leadership, despised both Li and Chang. But by specializing and experimenting in education, Chang would lead the way to abolishing the ancient examination system in 1905. He may become better appreciated as time goes on. Morse wrote of their first encounter:

> I expected to see a big burly man with a square head and found a frail looking man with an intellectual face and a long white Confucian beard. He seemed disappointed at my want of white hair and repeated a remark on the mature age of Mr. Moorhead and the help he had given. To this I replied that Mr. Moorhead was a man of ability which I could not hope to rival, but that I had had twenty-five years experience of Customs working and hoped that industry and application would enable me to make up for any natural deficiencies. This seemed to please him. I gave him your compliments as directed, and he inquired after your health. I said I had orders not to assume charge until I had finished work which he would entrust to me.[21]

This of course was an auspicious beginning for the customs commissioner, who had a job to do on behalf of Robert Hart within the jurisdiction of one of the chief officials of the Chinese Empire.

Morse's usefulness to the governor-general was immediately demonstrated at their first meeting, when arrangements for the reception of the German kaiser's brother, Prince Heinrich, had to be made. As latecomers to colonial empire in East Asia during the 1890s, the Germans seemed frighteningly pushy and demanding. By 1895 the proportion of German shipping in China's foreign trade had become second only to that of Britain, though actually about one-eighth in volume. Kaiser Wilhelm II wanted to make the area occupied by Germany at Tsingtao, Shantung, into a second Hong Kong. His brother, Prince Heinrich, sailed to China with German troops that landed in May 1898 to garrison the new Shantung leasehold. In September 1899 the prince broke ground for the new German railway that would penetrate from Tsingtao into the Chinese heartland. This was the portentous and formidable figure who now was descending upon the Wuhan cities, confident of the impending breakup of China.[22]

Morse's report to Hart on his first meeting with Chang Chih-tung
continued:

> First he said he wished me to call in his company on Prince Heinrich
> and the next day receive his return visit at Wu- ch'ang. He told me the
> salutes arranged to which I said that what was done at Tientsin and
> Nanking would be rightly done here: but he was much concerned at the
> use of the yellow chair provided by the Consul, fearing hooting by
> street urchins. I said it was the raising of an overt objection that would
> make the Germans absolutely determined to use yellow. He will send
> his carriage and a green chair with yellow tassels, leaving it to the
> Prince to choose either of those or the yellow chair of his own.[23]

In the end, the use of an honor guard of Ch'ing cavalry obviated the chair
question for Prince Heinrich. Nonetheless, Morse had demonstrated to
Chang one of the many ways in which Customs officers could help Chinese
officials avoid giving offense to the power-hungry imperialists, who were
then aiming to carve up the Chinese melon.

According to Morse, the governor-general "had very little to say about
Yochow." He merely noted that the taotai would "transfer his seat to Yochow
... and be Superintendent [of Customs]" and that "the procedure and regulations
adopted for Woosung would be applied to Yochow." Chang also promised to
supply Morse with a map and copies of all relevant documents. Hosea, for his
part, "thought it better to wait until I had seen the Taotai at Yochow before going
into much detail, but I stated as a general principle that it would be well for the
Taotai and Commissioner to act in conjunction for the municipality as for the
Customs and the more thoroughly this were done the less likely foreign powers
would be to demand exclusive concessions. He spoke of [local Chinese]
hostility and said the stupid people might make trouble but that *gentry* and
merchants all call for the opening of the port."[24]

After telling Hart that he had wired for the Woosung, Hangchow,
and Soochow regulations and had asked Neumann and Howard for their
notes on Yochow and Soochow, respectively, Morse went on to stress that
the location of the railway station at Yochow was a matter of critical
importance. As had been the case at Lungchow, "of the two sites possible
for steamers, one only may be possible for the railway." Thus, logistical
considerations might "absolutely determine the position of the settlement."
In closing he offered reassurance to his boss in Peking: "I shall feel my way,
say what ought to be done, impress on them my reasons, and leave the

responsibility on the Taotai—always with reference to the Viceroy in reserve." Meanwhile, as he waited for the Yochow arrangements to develop, Morse negotiated with the Hankow British Municipal Council in the British Concession to procure a well-situated building for the Customs at Hankow.[25]

Setting Up the New Port

In arranging for the establishment of a treaty port at Yochow, Morse had two major areas of concern, which he attempted to differentiate. One was creating the port itself; the other was promoting trade—in particular gaining acceptance for the shipping and new tariff regulations. As to the first, the site selected had to be on high ground, since most of the land on both sides of the Hsiang was subject to flooding during much of the year. The village of Ch'eng-lin, almost at the mouth of the Hsiang River and about five miles below the Yochow prefectural city, provided the best alternative. Furthermore, since this river was also the outlet for the vast Tung-t'ing Lake, the settlement would be at a choke point for controlling all river traffic, not only from Hunan but also from the south. Only here, Morse explained, "were found together the essential conditions of space for godowns and houses, sheltered anchorage, and a fair-sized creek giving a refuge for cargo boats."[26]

Along the shoreline of the village the site was surveyed for the building of a bund and a main street with lots that could be leased to foreign establishments. In the middle of the proposed bund, an area was assigned for the construction of a customshouse and staff quarters for the outdoor staff: "The land is high, fifteen to twenty feet above the bund, but terracing will make it as suitable as if it were on the level. For Commissioner's house and Indoor Staff quarters we have a piece of ground on low hills to the north of the Liu-king temple, some fifty feet above the ground level. Both sites should be airy and healthy."[27] Morse noted that since foreigners were not allowed to live in temples in Hunan, and since Ch'eng-lin had only two thousand people, initially the sole rental house available had to be for the commissioner, with room for two members of the indoor staff. The outdoor staff were temporarily assigned to live on two houseboats.[28] A little later he managed to rent houses for them.

Land and municipal regulations provided the constitutional under-pinning for the Ch'eng-lin settlement. Morse described the initial arrange-ments: "The Chinese government expropriated the land required for an

supply Chinese weaving of cotton goods, Morse pointed directly to the high costs of imported cotton goods from Manchester, Lowell, and Atlanta. This, he maintained, demonstrated how the thrifty Chinese peasant, when he finds the "price of what he desires beyond the limit which he considers within his means, throws his cheap labor into the scale and thereby alters the course of trade."[9]

With respect to tea production—recall his earlier advice to Ch'ing officials in both Taiwan and Hunan—Morse remarked that "the extreme subdivision of plantations and consequent multiplicity of interests," together with a short season for producing tea, put Chinese production behind that of British India. To remedy the situation, he advocated that Chinese tea guilds invest in the education of the growers and in advertising their product. The Ceylon tea planters, he argued, had invested heavily in promotion, whereas China's traders "do not yet realize the necessity of advertising." He suggested that Chinese producers "must tax themselves as the Indian planters have done" for these purposes. Morse concluded: "The Chinese tea traders can save the Chinese tea trade and no one else can."[10]

Another of the statistical secretary's insights concerned China's balance of payments—a subject with which Morse would earn his fame. His *Report on the Foreign Trade of China for 1903* posed the problem by noting a huge discrepancy between China's imports, estimated at 310 million taels, and Chinese exports, which he calculated to be 236 million taels. The next year Morse published *An Inquiry into the Commercial Liabilities and Assets of China in International Trade,* designed to explain how China could meet its heavy payments of loans and indemnities to the foreign powers despite the fact that Chinese imports had paradoxically increased until they were now "a third greater than the exports."[11] This question naturally preoccupied Hart's superiors in Peking. It was thus at the I.G.'s request that Morse tried to calculate all payments inward and outward that would affect China's fiscal situation.

He faced many difficulties with the data. Hong Kong, for instance, was a free port where trade figures might be ambiguously either local or international. Foreign firms often failed to report (or underreported) the profits they took out; and the Ch'ing government had no precise data on remittances sent back to China from overseas Chinese. Nonetheless, Morse managed to produce a large and comprehensive table of estimated assets and liabilities.

China's assets included exports of merchandise, shipments of bullion and coin, expenditures on the development of railways and mines, and outlays not only on foreign legations, consulates, and garrisons but also on the maintenance and repair of war and merchant vessels. Funds imported to maintain foreign missions, hospitals, and schools, expenditures by tourists, and remittances from immigrants abroad also counted as assets. Against these figures stood liabilities such as imported merchandise, bullion, and coin, principal and interest on loans and indemnities, expenditures for Chinese embassies and consulates abroad, money spent by Chinese students and travelers, net profits of foreigners remitted to home countries, costs of freight and insurance, and imported munitions of war. Nearly all these sums had to be in round figures—at the level of intelligent guesses rather than hard data.

Totaling his estimates, Morse arrived at liabilities of 423.7 million HK (*hai-kuan;* i.e., Customs) taels for liabilities and 424.7 million taels for assets. Except for merchandise, the largest single figure was the remittances from Chinese abroad, which he calculated at 73 million taels on the basis of extensive studies by a German of the total number of Chinese residing in foreign countries. Takeshi Hamashita, a well-known economic historian at the Institute of Oriental Culture at Tokyo University, points out that Morse was the first person to take into account these vast overseas Chinese remittances. Morse also broke new ground by considering the economic role of Hong Kong and the complex multilateral commerce with China that embraced not only the West but also India, Southeast Asia, Korea, and Japan. By so doing Morse proved that China's trade was much more in balance than had previously been perceived. He invented this approach, which remains a fundamental contribution.[12]

The balance of payments in China's foreign trade was a subject that had engaged the attention of many thoughtful administrators before Morse. Commissioner Dick at Shanghai in the 1860s and later Kopsch, Hippisley, Jenks, and others had tried their hand at it. Hart suggested that Morse get advice from Sir Charles Addis and introduced the vicomte d'Ollone to him for the same purpose. Morse also had to be mindful of the expressed interest of Ch'ing officials, notably Chao Erh-sun at the Board of Revenue (Hu-pu), and members of the new Board of Trade (Shang-pu). Later in the 1920s, when economist Charles F. Remer spent five years calculating China's foreign trade balance, he also settled upon the prime importance of Chinese remittances as the invisible hand that maintained equilibrium.[13] In effect, Morse's early estimates were the most comprehensive at the time and advanced the subject to a higher level of methodological sophistication.

Hart, who had his own ideas about format and details, provided considerable guidance to Morse in his early writing projects. He welcomed Morse's conclusions about China's balance of payments and the crucial role of "invisible" remittances by overseas Chinese. He also accepted Morse's analysis of Hong Kong's role within the framework of multilateral international trade. But Hart pushed the notion that the sums collected and paid to the bankers' commissions to meet indemnity and loan obligations did not actually leave the country. His reasoning was that payment of bullion into the banks did not lead to its shipment abroad. Such exports of funds were made in other ways, and the silver bullion (sycee) went back into circulation in China. Morse did not pick up this idea—probably because he thought it presented too superficial and optimistic a picture. As Hamashita observes, Morse remained objective about economics, whereas Hart sometimes tried to make his figures look better for China's sake.[14]

Hamashita emphasizes, however, that the effort by Morse and Hart to describe China's national economy was hindered by regional and local factors.[15] This was particularly true as Chinese administration became ever more decentralized in the early 1900s. Even the most rudimentary calculations involved substantial difficulties. In the first place, the enormous variation in the value of local currencies, and the use of copper, silver, and gold for different kinds of economic exchange, complicated all calculations. Furthermore, the increased autonomy of regional officials hindered efforts at centralized supervision and accounting. Many issues were slippery. For example, Chinese immigrants sent in money, but they represented at the same time lost labor. Moreover, these immigrants were a "regional" factor (the great majority were originally from South China) rather than a "national" one. Hong Kong presented a different kind of problem: in some respects it could be considered part of China, but in others it was essentially independent as a British colony.

Against the trend toward decentralization, the inspectorate general and consortia of foreign banks served as intermediaries, helping to integrate local and central offices as well as domestic and foreign trade interests. Although Morse did not fully understand the complex interplay of various centrifugal and centripetal forces operating in China, he nonetheless pioneered in defining the Chinese national economy, making possible more accurate conclusions about China's balance of payments. Moreover, from a professional standpoint his service at the Statistical Department marked his transition from a customs commissioner to a highly regarded specialist on the trade and administration of the Chinese Empire.

of the Chinese Government, especially in the development and improvement of the Bureau of Statistics—and also to activity and prominence in learned Societies in matters connected with the Far East. He lectures frequently before such societies in England—and his talks have a broader range, sometimes than their designation would lead one to expect."[71] Thwing, for his part, understood how much it all meant to Morse. On November 14, 1923, he confided to Merrill: "I think he once said to me, 'I would creep on my hands and knees from England to America, to get a Harvard LL.D.' Blessings on the dear man."[72]

With such devoted and enthusiastic support, Morse became the member of his class singled out for appropriate honor at the fiftieth reunion, and so he stood first among his surviving classmates. His career had begun at Harvard, and now he was honored there; to Hosea it was doubtless the crowning achievement of his life. President Lowell's citation provided a summary judgment of Morse's work: "Offered, on graduation here, a career in a foreign land, he rose to the highest distinction in the Chinese Customs Service. Notable authority on the nation that he served so long."[73] C.A.V. Bowra, then Customs nonresident secretary, sent a dispatch about Morse's honor to the current inspector-general, F.A. Aglen, who included it with his own circular to all the commissioners.

At this time Morse, who continued to smoke until about five years before his death, was regaining strength from a debilitating winter bout of bronchitis or pneumonia. Soon after receiving his honorary degree, he wrote to Thwing from Boston: "I have been ill and have not written my own letters for some time." Nonetheless, he was able to report that he "got the MS. of my book [the *Chronicles*], 4 vols., in to the publisher's hands just three days before I was taken ill. This is about the fifth private letter written with my own hand since the New Year."[74] By October 1924 he had recovered sufficiently to devote his energies to proofreading and indexing the *Chronicles,* and by late November he could announce: "My history is getting ready. I have just finished proofs of two (out of four) volumes, and have reason to hope that it may be out by next spring."[75]

This was not to be the case, however. Poor health returned, impeding the process of proofreading and forcing Morse to curtail many other activities as well. He stopped going into London for meetings and other purposes and no longer went out after sunset.[76] He had to resign from the Council of the Royal Asiatic Society and from committee duty at the University of London, and he was also obliged to give up the local Shakespeare Society, of which he had been "the guiding spirit."[77] Meanwhile, the arduous task of making final revisions, preparing, binding, and issuing four volumes totaling about sixteen hundred pages, not to mention unanticipated problems such as a porters' strike in the publishing trade, further delayed production.[78]

Finally, on April 26, 1926, Morse could tell Thwing, who by this time had retired as president of Western Reserve University, "My book is launched, and is well received. I hope you will have received your copy ere this. And I too am now Emeritus and my weapon is now the wooden sword."[79] Although Morse claimed to be pleased with the volumes' initial reception, in July he remained anxious over the absence of "American press notices up to this date." Positive reviews had come in from England, India, and China, he said, "but none yet from America." Morse then permitted himself a rare moment of self-congratulation: "[O]ne of my friends writes to me that the book has been a veritable gold-mine to him: he has contributed reviews of it to two weeklies, two monthlies and a quarterly."[80]

Morse dedicated his monumental four-volume work "To the memory of Edward B. Drew with grateful recollection of our friendship of fifty years." But he also obviously appreciated Thwing's loyalty and support, and he graciously arranged for a copy of the *Chronicles* to be sent to him "in humble recognition of the many merits which I may admire but cannot hope to imitate, and as a mark of my sense of your many kindnesses. Make the most of this, for then I shall have written myself out. We write with one voice to send you both our best love."[81]

As events unfolded, the discovery of additional East India Company records in the British Legation in Peking provided Morse with material for a fifth volume, which he completed about two years after the first four. On March 11, 1928, he told Thwing that this new material allowed him "to fill an eighteenth century gap (of three decades)," adding that "now I really have finished with the writing of books."[82]

Morse's Last Years

Morse found substantial enjoyment in the twilight of his life. He relished discussions of scholarship and politics with neighbors and took special pleasure in visits from longtime friends. Merrill dropped in once or twice on his way to visit his daughter (who was married to a Customs officer in China), and Dana never failed to look Hosea up during his yearly sojourns in England. Nan's relatives, including Dora and Henry Pancoast, also occasionally made their way to Arden. When Nan's niece Anne Welsford began studying at Cambridge University, Hosea took a particular interest in her life and became an adopted uncle to her three roommates. His letters to Anne, then known as "Anon," were affectionate, playful, and reminiscent. She later speculated that "it was my youth which pleased him the most. He was always young at heart."[83]

Nan Morse seems to have maintained several close relationships at Camberley, despite her erratic personality and "ungovernable fits of passion."[84] According to Anne Welsford, "My aunt had a number of elderly friends, Miss Keightley & Miss Chaplin, Mrs. Michelmore & her daughter, Miss Jameson and others. When my mother was staying at 'Arden' she liked to send her round to call on them with little bunches of flowers. Otherwise they came to her. She [Nan] didn't go out much because she . . . [suffered from] ill health." It is doubtful that any of Hosea's Chinese acquaintances came to call. Certainly we have no record of such a visit. Nan remained hostile to the Chinese until her death and, Anne Welsford said, "would not have welcomed a Chinaman at 'Arden.' "[85]

Although Morse seems to have been perfectly content to spend the last two decades of his life as a British subject living in England, he nonetheless reached out to confirm his American heritage near the end. In 1929, for instance, he became a corresponding member of the Colonial Society of Massachusetts. This was not a pro forma matter, however. In fact, it required a long letter of explanation as to why neither he nor his wife had birth certificates. Eventually things worked out, and in accepting his membership Morse took pains to express his "sense of the honour which has been conferred upon me and my acceptance of it."[86]

During the last ten years of his life Morse did not write as frequently to his longtime friend Charles F. Thwing as he had done earlier. Still, he valued Thwing's letters—in part, no doubt, because Thwing so thoroughly and obviously appreciated Hosea's scholarly talents. In two particularly revealing letters, Morse provides us with a rare description of his approach to the writing of history. The first is dated October 11, 1925. "In my history," he says, "I tried to give a plain narrative of the absolute facts, such that, by judicious selection, both sides could find ammunition for their causes—for no cause was ever so bad that there was nothing to be said in its favour. . . . I am no good as a prophet: I follow the maxim—'never prophesy unless you know'; and the ordinary American audience wants to know, not what happened yesterday, but what is going to happen tomorrow; they seem unwilling to make the mental exertion to judge tomorrow by yesterday."[87]

Three and a half years later, on April 25, 1929, we find Morse

responding to one of Thwing's letters of praise. He begins with characteristic modesty: "You are too generous in your comments on my writings.
My only merit is that I saw a field which had not been properly cultivated
and I stepped in and plowed deeper."[88] Then he offers a cogent analysis of
the impact of his scholarly work:

> Now that my job is finished I find myself confronted with two
> opposing influences. One is the extreme nationalist view and its up-
> holders: my history of the last century was written without bias and as
> a contribution to serious history, without many adjectives or epithets.
> This does not meet the views of the nationalists, and they have put on
> the "index" a condensation by MacNair of my three volumes, brought
> down by him to 1928. An edition of 1000 has been withdrawn and
> suppressed on demand of the students and the government. MacNair
> knows China well and has the historian's mind; he was a long time at
> St. John's (Shanghai) and is now at the Univ. of Chicago. He refuses
> to budge and so do I.[89]

"The other influence," Morse goes on to say, "wishes to dig deeper than I
have done. From a friend I have received an intimation that the Harvard
Business School will apply for my help in securing records of trade at
Canton in the early days. For the English trade all surviving records are in
the India Office, available for students working there. I know of no others,
but those I have studied very thoroughly, and I have had the student of
economics and finance constantly in mind; he will find much information
in my five volumes 1635–1834 with the aid of the index."[90]

It was, of course, Morse's reputation as a talented and objective
China scholar that drew John Fairbank to become his disciple as a Rhodes
Scholar in 1930. He often visited Morse and appreciated his guidance and
expertise. After Fairbank went to China, they continued an affectionate
correspondence until Hosea's death from pneumonia on February 13, 1934.

Morse's demise brought expressions of sympathy and testimonials
of praise from all parts of the world. When Hosea's niece Janet heard that
he had died, she wrote her estranged aunt a long and generous letter, which
read in part:

> It is hard to express in mere words how very deeply I sympathize
> with you. I know you meant a great deal to each other and life for either
> of you without the other must be hard to contemplate. . . . I feel a great
> sense of loss too for no one could have received better care and attention

than you and Uncle gave me and I am not ungrateful though I may have appeared so. I have thought of you both more than you could imagine. I have told my children about Uncle Hose [*sic*] what a wonderful man he was, and how they could wish for nothing better than that they could be like him.[91]

Nan, who apparently never answered the letter directly, died six years later.[92]

On Sunday, February 25, 1934, John Fairbank wrote the following obituary notice for the editorial page of the *Peiping Chronicle:*

The death of Dr. Hosea Ballou Morse, announced on February 20, marked the passing of an historian of the rarest calibre, the preeminent value of whose work is only beginning to be generally appreciated.

"The International Relations of the Chinese Empire" has long been accepted as a standard work, remarkable for its breadth of scope and accuracy of detail, and indispensable in a field of history in which only the main outlines of historical fact are as yet known. But it may be questioned if many readers, among the thousands who have used these volumes for constant reference, have realized the intellectual triumph which they represent or the romance which lies behind their many footnotes.

The fact is that Dr. Morse lived through two full and crowded careers, each of them a life of achievement in itself. For thirty-five years, from 1874 to 1908, he served under Sir Robert Hart in the Chinese Maritime Customs, playing an active and trusted part in the building up of the Service and contributing to the development of modern China. For a score of years thereafter, changing from the making to the writing of history, he did again the work of a pioneer. With persistent industry in the face of precarious health, and with an insight born of rich experience, he was able to weave from the many and tangled threads of Tsing [Ch'ing] Dynasty foreign relations a masterpiece of historical writing. In doing so he advanced by many years, perhaps by decades, the study of modern Chinese history.

Such an achievement was possible because of the complete accuracy and personal impartiality of the writer's mind. The same desire for established fact which made Dr. Morse invaluable as a Statistical Secretary made him preeminent as an historian. Revision and correction of his work, of the imperfection of which he was all too humbly aware, will continue from year to year, together with the elaboration of subjects which he only touched upon in passing. But it may safely be

Notes

Abbreviations

AW	Anne Welsford
CFT	Charles F. Thwing
DL	Dana Family Letters, Massachusetts Historical Society, Boston
HBM	Hosea Ballou Morse
HFM	H.F. Merrill family letters, in the possession of his granddaughter Rosamund B. Beasley, of Chatham, Mass.
HFML	H.F. Merrill letter books, Houghton Library, Harvard Univ.
JKF	John King Fairbank
MC	Morse Collection, letters from Hart to his commissioners, Houghton Library, Harvard Univ.
MHC	Martha Henderson Coolidge
ML	Morse Letter Books, pressed copies of Morse's semiofficial letters to Hart and others, Houghton Library, Harvard Univ.
MP	Morse Papers (miscellaneous content, mostly correspondence and personal records), in the possession of MHC
MS	Morse Scrapbook (undergraduate materials and later materials to 1879), Harvard Univ. Archives, Pusey Library
NCH	*North China Herald*
RH	Robert Hart
SL	Spinney Letters, Peabody and Essex Museum Library, Salem, Mass.
TC	Thwing Collection, classification 1DD6, personal papers of CFT, Box 29, correspondence with Morse, by permission of Case Western Reserve Univ. Archives

Introduction

1. MP: HBM to JKF, Dec. 19, 1931.
2. Fairbank, *Trade and Diplomacy on the China Coast,* dedication.

3. Fairbank, Bruner, and Matheson, eds., *I.G. in Peking;* Bruner, Fairbank, and Smith, eds., *Entering China's Service;* Smith, Fairbank, and Bruner, eds., *Robert Hart and China's Early Modernization.*

1
Origins and Education, 1855-1874

1. For genealogies, see MP: tables by HBM, edited by Janet Morse Donnelly et al.; also Cleveland, comp., *Genealogy of the Cleveland and Cleaveland Families,* 3 vols. nos. 1234 and 3635; The Rev. Abner Morse, *General Register of . . . Sherburn and Holliston;* J. Howard Morse and Emily W. Leavitt, comps., *Morse Genealogy,* 2 vols. sec. Z, nos. 476, 1053, 1054, 1066, 2250, and pp. 150 and 153; and esp. Fred E. Crowell, "New Englanders in Nova Scotia," unpublished, copyrighted manuscript. In Crowell, each family, listed by number, is traced back to the original New England pioneers; Morse's family number is 526.
2. John King Fairbank's ancestor, Jonathan Fairebanke, was Samuel Morse's companion in founding Dedham. The house they built is now advertised as "the oldest house in America" (Fairbanks, *Genealogy of the Fairbanks Family,* 31).
3. MP: HBM to H.F. MacNair, Dec. 26, 1931; William V. Morse to HBM, Oct. 10, 1907. MacNair taught at St. John's University, Shanghai, and later at the University of Chicago. He and Fairbank planned a biography of Morse, for which Morse wrote an autobiographical report. The Morse Papers include a "chronology" and career résumés up to 1924.
4. Crowell, "New Englanders in Nova Scotia," no. 526. The Acadians were a separate group from the French in Quebec. They were the first European settlers of Acadia (the modern maritime provinces) and had been there since the early 1600s. Champlain had explored and charted Acadia, setting up a fort at Port Royal (near Annapolis Royal) in 1605. The British felt they could not trust the Acadians and preferred Protestant, English-speaking settlers.
5. MacVicar, *Short History of Annapolis Royal,* 98-99: "One hundred acres were to be allowed each settler, and fifty acres to every member of his family, on condition that the land be cultivated in thirty years." See also Crowell, "New Englanders in Nova Scotia," no. 526; Stewart and Rawlyk, *People Highly Favored of God,* 4; E.C. Wright, *Planters and Pioneers,* 198; Robert R. McLeod, "Annapolis," 265-73.
6. McLeod, "Northern Queens, Nova Scotia," 104-57; see also MacVicar, *Short History of Annapolis Royal,* 99.
7. McLeod, "Annapolis," 273.
8. Crowell, "New Englanders in Nova Scotia," no. 526 (Morse family), no. 165 (Church family), no. 76 (Chipman family), no. 272 (Hicks family), nos. 301-3 (Dexter families), no. 110 (Cleveland family); Cleveland, comp., *Genealogy of the Cleveland and Cleaveland Families;* J. Howard Morse and Leavitt,

comps., *Morse Genealogy.* Anna Church, wife of Abner Morse (1731-1803), was the daughter of Jonathan and Thankful Bullard Church of Watertown, next to Cambridge. David Chipman Morse (1777-1843) married Hannah Hicks, daughter of John and Sarah Church Hicks.

9. Rawlyk, *Nova Scotia's Massachusetts,* 22-24.
10. MacVicar, *Short History of Annapolis Royal,* 99.
11. William Inglis Morse, *Gravestones of Acadie,* 15.
12. Crowell, "New Englanders in Nova Scotia," no. 526.
13. MP: HBM to Perkin (presumably of the Colonial Society of Massachusetts), Dec. 9, 1928.
14. McLeod, "Northern Queens, Nova Scotia," 147, 151-52; MacLeod, "Nova Scotian Gains Distinction Abroad," 9. Alice MacLeod came from Caledonia, Queens County, a little town next to South Brookfield. Consequently, she knew all about Morse's family.
15. Apparently the earlier generations favored "Parks", but cousins of Morse's with the middle name used "Park."
16. *T.B. Smith, Genealogies,* MG 1, vol. 850, pp. 11, 248, 646, 800, 896; *Queen's County Genealogies,* MG 4, vol. 131, pp. 190-92; McLeod, "Northern Queens, Nova Scotia," 152-53.
17. MacLeod, "Nova Scotian Gains Distinction Abroad," 9.
18. Miller, *Larger Hope,* 41. The Universalist membership included occasional Anglicans and lapsed Congregationalists, plus Baptists, Methodists, and Quakers. See also Eddy, *Universalism in America,* 2:482. Eddy feared the influence of German spiritualism.
19. Ballou, *Biography of Rev. Hosea Ballou by His Youngest Son,* 61.
20. G.H. Williams, "American Universalism," 9, 13.
21. Watts, "Man Spelled Large," 4. See also Hewett, *Unitarians in Canada,* 80-85; and Miller, *Larger Hope,* 688-89.
22. MacLeod, "Nova Scotian Gains Distinction Abroad," 9.
23. MP: HBM to JKF, Sept. 3, 1931.
24. Universalist-Unitarian Church of Halifax, Records.
25. News of the deaths of his younger brothers apparently came to Hosea indirectly, if at all. His uncle, William V. Morse, wrote him from Omaha on October 25, 1907, mentioning, "[D]id you know that Ernest died at Hartford last summer. Natural causes." Another uncle, John L. McIntosh, wrote on March 10, 1915: "I presume, no doubt, you have heard of your brother, Harvie's death" (letters in MP). About Albert, nothing was said. Even his daughter did not know when he died.
26. MP: letter from HBM's first cousin, Olivia Hunt, in Brookfield, to their uncle, John L. McIntosh, in Boston, Jan. 18, 1915. James B. Hunt, a blacksmith, boarded with the Brydens at the time. When Olivia Hunt wrote to ask if he remembered Morse's birth, he replied, "Well I think I ought to there being no

Afterword

1. On Morse's effort to seek intellectual renewal through the minds of the young, see TC: HBM to CFT, Aug. 18, 1932.
2. MP: JKF to Lindsay Pancoast Zimmerman, Sept. 19, 1988.
3. Ibid. See also MP: AW to Lindsay Pancoast Zimmerman, June 15, 1973.
4. MP: AW to MHC, Nov. 26, 1989.
5. See, for example, MP: Lindsay Pancoast Zimmerman to JKF, Aug. 2, 1988; also Sarah Welsford to Janet Morse Donnelly, July 24, 1934.
6. MP: AW to MHC, Dec. 2, 1989.
7. MP: Janet Morse tapes, 1981-82.
8. MP: AW to MHC, Nov. 26, 1989.
9. MP: JKF to Lindsay Pancoast Zimmerman, Oct. 6, 1988. See also chapter 11, note 13.
10. MP: Janet Morse tapes, 1981-82.
11. MP: JKF to Lindsay Pancoast Zimmerman, Nov. 25, 1988.
12. Before this point we have no clear contemporary evidence of Nan's instability. Janet's tape-recorded recollections of 1981-82, although extremely valuable in many respects, are disjointed and therefore unreliable from the standpoint of chronology. Cf. note 13 below.
13. MP: AW to MHC, Jan. 24, 1990. See also Lal (Nan's youngest sister) to Janet, Feb. 28, 1934: "[Nan] was always a borderline case but I am not sure she hasn't stepped across."
14. MP: Lindsay Pancoast Zimmerman to JKF, Nov. 2, 1988; AW to MHC, Jan. 24, 1990.
15. MP: AW to MHC, Dec. 2, 1989, and Jan. 24 and Feb. 6, 1990.
16. See MP: AW to MHC, Jan. 24, 1990. For Nan's paranoid response to Fairbank, see Evans, *John Fairbank and the American Understanding of Modern China,* 36. A note by Fairbank dated December 1986 refers to some letters that had been removed from Morse's files, "to be copied for Mrs. Morse (AJM) as part of her campaign after his death to prove that I had misused materials he gave me."
17. See Dana's account of his London lunch with Morse on June 28, 1926, in which he remarks that "this time I felt a strong affection for him as well as admiration." Dana, "Journal . . . of R.H. Dana III and his second wife in the Massachusetts Historical Society Archives.
18. MP: AW to MHC, Nov. 26, 1989. See also AW to Lindsay Pancoast Zimmerman, June 15, 1973, and AW to MHC, Jan. 24 and Feb. 6, 1990.
19. MP: AW to MHC, Nov. 26, 1989.
20. Compare Bruner, Fairbank, and Smith, eds., *Entering China's Service,* 330; and TC: HBM to CFT, July 14, 1908. See also MP: HBM to JKF, Feb. 4, 1932.
21. Note especially her remark to Fairbank in his *Chinabound,* 20.

22. MP: AW to JKF, Feb. 22, 1987.

23. See Smith, Fairbank, and Bruner, eds., *Robert Hart and China's Early Modernization;* and HBM, "Repayment by the West of Its Debt to the East," 134.

24. For examples of Morse's bibliographic advice, see MP: HBM to JKF, Jan. 25, Feb. 4, and June 5, 1932.

25. Perhaps Morse's long experience in the British-dominated Chinese Customs, together with his own history as a British subject, predisposed Morse toward British sources.

26. Dennett, *Americans in Eastern Asia,* 690.

27. For these and other criticisms, consult, for example, Rowe, *Hankow;* and Hao, *Commercial Revolution in Nineteenth-Century China.*

28. Fairbank, *Great Chinese Revolution,* ix.

29. MP: HBM to JKF, Nov. 1, 1930.

30. MP: HBM to JKF, March 1, 1931.

31. TC: HBM to CFT, Aug. 6, 1922. See also Cohen and Goldman, comps., *Fairbank Remembered,* 113-14, 119-20; Evans, *John Fairbank and the American Understanding of Modern China,* 16.

32. MP: HBM to JKF, April 17, 1933. See also Sept. 22, 1932, p. 77.

33. See, for example, MP: JKF to HBM, March 3, June 19, 1932, etc.

34. MP: HBM to JKF, Jan. 24, 1931, p. 23; July 13, 1933. See also Evans, *John Fairbank and the American Understanding of Modern China,* 52.

35. MP: HBM to JKF, Sept. 20, 1932; see also Cohen and Goldman, comps., *Fairbank Remembered,* 57, 79, 99, 104, etc.

36. MP: HBM to JKF, Dec. 19, 1931.

37. MP: JKF to HBM, June 19, 1932; HBM to JKF, July 14, 1932.

38. MP: HBM to JKF, July 26, 1933.

39. Evans, *John Fairbank and the American Understanding of Modern China,* xiv.

40. See ibid., 329, for another view.

41. Ibid., 20; MP: HBM to JKF, Dec. 12, 1932.

42. Cohen and Goldman, comps., *Fairbank Remembered,* 132.

43. Evans, *John Fairbank and the American Understanding of Modern China,* 38; Fairbank, *Chinabound,* 95.

44. MP: HBM to JKF, Dec. 19, 1931; Cohen and Goldman, comps., *Fairbank Remembered,* 226.

45. See MP: HBM to JKF, Dec. 22, 1932, p. 78; Cohen and Goldman, comps., *Fairbank Remembered,* 104.

46. Fairbank, *Chinabound,* 447.

47. Cohen and Goldman, comps., *Fairbank Remembered,* 123.

48. TC: HBM to CFT, Nov. 28, 1921.

Bibliographic Notes

John K. Fairbank

The Value of the Customs Correspondence

One of the great untapped reservoirs of information on the economy, finances, and politics of late imperial China is the file of English-language letters from the commissioners to the inspector-general. Only after Hart's retirement were there Chinese commissioners of customs. Each of the thirty to forty commissioners at the treaty ports wrote a more or less fortnightly personal, semiofficial letter to the I.G., summarizing under various headings the events and problems of the commissioner's work. These included personal reports of interviews with Chinese officials as well as the economic and political situation in general. The commissioner would report especially upon his contact with the chief officials of the region, to whom he served usually as an adviser with reference particularly to taxation, to development of trade and industries, including mining, and to relations with foreign consuls in the local scene. The customs commissioner, in short, was a foreign employee of the Chinese government who did not claim high status in the local official hierarchy but rather a special status as a channel of contact with Hart at Peking. Most commissioners seemed to have acquired from Robert Hart a wide interest in projects for development and modernization. The result of this type of correspondence, in addition to the official dispatches of the Customs Service, was to give Hart his own network of intelligence from all over the empire.

The half dozen or more series of special monographs in the Customs publication program, as well as the *Returns of Trade* and the *Decennial Reports,* have long been relied upon as important sources for the late nineteenth century. The Customs archives that were collected in the 1930s